PASSING
THE TEST

A GUIDE FOR THE IRISH LEARNER DRIVER

Dominic McGinley

MENTOR

First Published 1988 by Borderline Publications.
Published and reprinted by Anna Livia Press
1989, 1990, 1991, 1992, 1993, 1995

First published by Mentor Books in 1996
Revised Edition 1999
© Dominic McGinley, 1999

3 5 7 9 10 8 6 4 2

ISBN: 0 947548 80 7

Author's Acknowledgements

My sincere thanks to my wife, Moya, for her unfailing encouragement throughout the preparation and re-working of this book. Special thanks to Chris Heffernan, who trained me in driving instruction; to Donal Moriarty, recently retired from the Driver Testing Section of the Department of the Environment; to Gerard Maher, Bernard Behan and John Harte, also of the Driver Testing Section and to the Press Officers of the D.O.E. for giving so generously of their time. Thanks to Tony Herron (Driving Instructor) for his encouragement. Sincere thanks to Garda Inspector P. O'Malley for information on road traffic law. Thanks to David Lambe of Alexandra School of Motoring for his support. Thanks to Tom Kerrigan and Derek Farrell of the Disabled Drivers Association of Ireland for their help. **Very special thanks to Mr. Gerard Maher, Principal Officer, Driver Control Section, Department of Environment for permission to reproduce road-signs from the *Rules of the Road*.**

Thanks also to Appleyard Car Sales Ltd. for the front cover photograph.

Biographical Note

Dominic McGinley was born in Dublin in 1954. He is a schoolteacher who has trained as a driving instructor. He has a keen interest in educational trends and has a special interest in text and readability studies. He is co-author and illustrator of two successful educational handbooks and regularly writes articles for a number of periodicals. He lives on Dublin's Northside.

Contents

PART 3   On the Road

PART 4   Test Manoeuvres

PART 5   Your Driving Test

Foreword

Passing the Test was written to help you as you prepare for your Driving Test. It is designed to allay any fears you might have about 'The Test', and to give you confidence as you prepare for a lifetime of safe motoring. It is not an interpretation of the law. It is merely a guide for the learner driver. It will give you an overview of the skills you need to pass your Driving Test. *Passing the Test* cannot, of course, take the place of an instructor or real driving experience.

Passing the Test was first published in late 1988. Since then more than 75,000 copies have been sold. From the positive feedback I have had, a considerable number of learner drivers have used it to good effect as they took – *and passed* – their Driving Test.

This updated text takes account of the current edition of the *Rules of the Road* booklet* and I recommend *Passing the Test* as a companion volume. There are numerous cross-references to the *Rules of the Road* booklet throughout the text which, I hope, will increase your knowledge and understanding of what to expect and what will be expected of you as you prepare for the *big day!*

Driving Tests are conducted by experienced and qualified officials of the Department of the Environment. Contrary to popular belief there are no failure quotas. Your task is to show that you are capable of handling your vehicle with confidence and competence. You must do this with proper regard for your own safety and the safety of other road users. At the same time you must put the Rules of the Road into practice.

Many drivers approach the test as if they were bound to fail. However, if you make adequate preparation, learn the Rules of the Road and take the time to learn to drive properly, then you should pass the Test. I hope that you will find this book useful as you prepare for – and pass – *your* Driving Test!

Dominic McGinley
April 1999

---

* Wherever you see ⛛ROTR you should refer to the specified page or pages in the *Rules Of The Road,* which is available at all Post Offices. Price £2.

Part 1: The Learner Driver

About Learner Drivers

Until you have passed your driving test you are still a learner driver. This means that if you drive a car, a van, a bus or a truck, you must display L plates on the front and rear of your vehicle. These must be at least (6in) 15cm high, and be red on a white background. Motorcycles and work-vehicles, such as tractors, are exempted from displaying L plates.

You must hold a provisional licence for the category of vehicle you drive. Licences are not transferrable and you are limited to the categories on your licence. For some licence categories you must already have a full licence for a smaller/lighter vehicle, before you will be granted a provisional licence for that category. If in doubt, ask at your local Motor Taxation Office. ▽ROTR 5, 6 & 7

During the period of your first and third provisional licences, you are required to be accompanied by a driver who holds a full licence for that category of vehicle. In this way you are encouraged to pass your driving test *before* your second provisional licence expires. This gives you up to four years to prepare for and pass your test. Really there is no reason why you should not pass your driving test within the first year of your first provisional licence! You cannot obtain a third or subsequent provisional licence unless you have undergone the driving test within the previous two years. Road tax and insurance are essential legal requirements and it is your responsibility to ensure that you have proper cover. If in doubt – check it out! ▽ROTR 8

Learning to Drive

Learner drivers often have to suffer the impatience and bad manners shown by 'qualified' drivers. Unfortunately, on Irish roads, courtesy and consideration are not as common as they ought to be. Learning any new skill can be very trying. This is particularly true of learning to drive. So, be prepared for the way others behave. When you have passed *your* test don't forget how much learner drivers have to contend with. Show them extra consideration!

When learning to drive you may find that, at times, you are full of confidence and carry out every instruction perfectly. At other times you may feel that you have forgotten everything you have been taught and that you should give up altogether. But don't despair! Learning to drive takes time and practice.

It has been estimated that most learner drivers need between 25 and 35 hours of motoring experience before being ready for the test. Some learners, however, will take a longer (others a shorter) time to master all the skills required to gain a Certificate of Competency.

Your driving experience should include all types of motoring situations. If you usually drive in country areas, then don't forget to get some city driving practice – and vice versa. There are almost fifty Driver Testing Centres around the country which are situated in various towns and cities, so you will need some driving practice in built up areas. Avoiding difficult driving situations could ensure failure in the test.

Learner drivers must develop a good attitude from the outset. Recognise your own limitations and remember that excessive speed, recklessness or trying to teach another road user 'a lesson' can end in tragedy. Don't let anything take your attention from the road and avoid anything which interferes with your reactions or slows them down. ▽ROTR 14

Plan your strategy for learning to drive. Once you have your provisional licence, decide when you intend to take the test. Set yourself a realistic target. You should be ready to take the test within a year of starting to drive. The longer you put off taking the test, the more difficult it will seem to you.

Motoring Schools – Professional Tuition

Most learner drivers prefer to start their driving career with a school of motoring. This is very wise, as you have the security of knowing that your instructor will have dual-control pedals and an understanding of your needs as a learner driver. You will also become familiar with the idea of taking instruction, i.e. someone *telling* you what to do.

When you approach a school of motoring for the first time, you may not know what to expect. You will require a vehicle which will suit *your* needs. Some driving schools use cars with diesel engines, others petrol or LPG. There is a distinct difference between the 'moving off' capability of a diesel engine as opposed to a petrol/gas engine, so consistency of vehicle is most important! Check out the cost and duration of lessons and be prepared to take *at least* 10 lessons in reasonably close succession. You may consider that this will prove expensive, but it is an investment in your driving career. Some driving schools offer special rates for a series of beginner's lessons.

Some motoring schools expect you to go to them, while others will arrange to pick you up. Some lessons last only 45 minutes, while others last a full hour. Weekend lessons may cost more than weekday lessons. Go on the recommendation of others and remember that you are paying for a service, so be choosy. If you are not satisfied – go elsewhere!

There are many schools of motoring to choose from. Look in the Golden Pages for an extensive list and pick one to suit your needs.

Qualified Instructors

Many schools of motoring are affiliated to the Motor Schools Association of Ireland (MSAI), whose aim is to increase the standard of driver education and to promote road safety. This organisation has a voluntary register of approved driving instructors (ADIR) which ensures the training and certification of instructors.

Consistency of instruction is essential, so try to arrange your lessons with the same instructor *every* time. In this way your instructor will be familiar with your progress and will ensure that you follow a developmental learning programme. Large motoring schools may have some difficulty in always providing you with the same instructor, as s/he may be in continuous demand. Make reasonable allowances for this.

All teachers have a different method and approach. The type of instruction given by a particular instructor may not suit your needs as a learner. Many learners go on the recommendation of others, but if you feel that you are not making satisfactory progress within a reasonable time, then change instructors. You shouldn't feel intimidated or antagonised by your instructor.

Good instructors are reliable and punctual. They will not over-estimate your ability and will not put you into situations beyond your competence. They will always give good example when they are driving or demonstrating, encouraging you and building your confidence, while helping you to develop the right attitude. They will allow you to take control of the vehicle, but will be able to take over control, if the need arises. They will also explain the driving errors of others, as well as correcting yours.

When you first begin to drive, you will probably be very tense and nervous. This is perfectly understandable and you should consider taking a single lesson at a time. As you gain confidence, double lessons may prove very useful, especially as you approach the date of your test. It is also advisable to arrange some pre-test lessons to ensure that you have everything just right! You should do this *at least* two weeks before the test date, as your instructor *may* have to advise you to postpone your test. Trust your instructor's experience and act on his or her advice.

Instruction from a Non-Professional

Since the Road Traffic Act of 1968, the Government has had the right to regulate the giving of driving instruction for reward. However, up to the time of publication, no such regulations have yet been drawn up or implemented. This means that, at present, it is not necessary to have a special qualification to give driving lessons; having a full licence is sufficient!

Not everyone, though, is good at imparting information or knowledge. It must be said that *some* learner drivers pass the test after good and careful instruction from a friend or relation who is not a professional instructor. If you have confidence in your instructor, then you *may* consider taking instruction from a non-professional.

Some learner drivers choose to combine professional and non-professional instruction. Since you must be accompanied by a suitably qualified driver during the period of your first and third provisional licences, you may benefit from their advice and experience, even if you are getting professional instruction. There is no shortcut to experience and everyone can benefit from good advice. Observing the driving of others, while mentally rehearsing what you would do if you were behind the wheel, can be useful, but if the driver you're observing has bad driving habits, they may mislead you.

One reason why you might choose *not* to take instruction from a friend or relative is that an argument could develop at a critical moment in traffic. This could prove dangerous! Only you can judge whether or not this kind of instruction will be valuable. Ultimately, the choice is yours!

Caveat

Some words of caution, though: *Do not try to teach yourself!* Any motor vehicle can be a lethal weapon, and your safety and the safety of others depends on your ability to control your vehicle properly. Your lack of experience could have fatal consequences! You have legal responsibilities too!

Why Do a Driving Test?

Irish drivers pay dearly for motor insurance. Provisional licence holders pay much more than full licence holders. So, if having a full driving licence means cheaper insurance, then why not do the driving test as soon as possible? There's also a great sense of achievement in passing your driving test. With proper instruction, adequate preparation and plenty of practice you should pass first time.

Applying for a Provisional Licence and a Driving Test

If you have no previous driving experience you may only apply for a provisional licence [Form D.301] for a motorcycle less than 125cc.(Category A1); for a motor car (Category B), for a van or small truck (Category C1) or a work vehicle (Category W). Local Authorities issue driving licences. Certain disabilities automatically disqualify a person from holding a licence, although some illnesses/disabilities will not cause disqualification if the applicant provides appropriate medical certificates.

Further details are to be found on the application form. You are required to submit your birth certificate and an eyesight report [Form D.509] with your application for a first provisional licence. The same report covers the driving test application form [Form D.401].

The application form [Form D.401] for a Certificate of Competency – the driving test – should include a contact telephone number, if at all possible. Special arrangements may have to be made for your driving test, e.g. in the case of disability, and many driver testing centres cannot provide driving tests for heavy goods vehicles (HGVs) or public service vehicles (PSVs). You will be informed of the nearest suitable test centre. If you live very far from the regular test centres and wish to undergo a motorcycle or work-vehicle test, then the Driver Testing Section will arrange your test at a town convenient to you.

The current fee for the driving test in categories A1, A, B, EB or W is £30. For categories C1, C, D1, or D it is £50 and for E category vehicles (other than EB) it is £60. These fees reflect the cost of administering the test. Send your completed form and the appropriate fee to:

Driver Testing Section,
Department of the Environment,
Government Buildings,
Ballina, Co. Mayo
Tel: 096 70677   Fax: 096 70680

Motor Schools Association of Ireland
email: msainews@iol.ie

Waiting Lists and Cancellations

At present, the average waiting time before being called for a test is 28 weeks; more from some centres. You may choose to reduce the waiting time further by stating that you are willing to take a cancellation, if it arises. Either way, you will receive an appointment slip confirming the date, time and place of your test approximately four weeks before your test.

Should you need to cancel your test appointment, you must give at least 10 working days notice or risk losing your fee. You may only postpone your test twice before your fee is forfeited. Previously there was no limit to the number of times you could cancel your test without penalty. If you forfeit your test fee you will have to re-apply and take your turn on the waiting list.

Driver Test Cancellation Answering Service
at 096 70809 24 hours a day, 7 days a week
or 01 6793200 ext. 428 (office hours only)

The Driving Test Schedule

The driving test consists of an oral test of the applicant's knowledge of the Rules of the Road and a practical test in driving by the applicant. The vehicle used must be representative of the category for which the application for a Certificate of Competency is made.

The following is a summary of the provisions made under the Road Traffic (Licensing of Drivers) Regulations, 1989. It provides a checklist of the skills which you will be expected to acquire in order to pass your driving test.

The driver tester must be satisfied that the applicant has a satisfactory knowledge of the Rules of the Road and can satisfactorily carry out any or all of the following operations:

- Starting and stopping the engine.
- Moving off, (straight ahead and at an angle) on uphill or downhill slopes.
- Meeting with, moving with and overtaking other traffic.
- Taking left-hand and right-hand turnings, and crossing intersections.
- Stopping the vehicle at various speeds including an emergency stop.*
- Parking the vehicle (other than a motorcycle) on uphill and downhill slopes, and oblique (not straightforward) parking.
- Causing the vehicle to face in the opposite direction using the steering, gears and brakes (Turnabout).
- Reversing a vehicle in a straight line and around corners. This does not include motorcycles.
- Giving signals of intended actions, by hand or by the use of direction indicators.
- Complying with signals for the control of traffic and taking appropriate action on meeting traffic signs and other authorised signs.

While carrying out these operations you must comply satisfactorily with the Rules of the Road and competently handle your vehicle without danger to others and with due regard for the safety and convenience of others.

* Although contained in the schedule, this is not yet a compulsory test manoeuvre.

16

Part 2: Taking Control

Your Vehicle (the POWER test)

First things first! You need a vehicle which is in roadworthy condition. Get into the habit of carrying out the **POWER** test before *every* run.

P – Petrol, gas or diesel.
O – Check the oil level, especially before long trips.
W – Water for engine-cooling and for windscreens.
E – Electrics, i.e. lights, horn, windscreen wipers etc.
R – Rubber. Tyres require a minimum tread of 1.6 mm. and correct pressure. Check your brakes too!

When you go for your test you will be required to sign an undertaking that the vehicle is roadworthy. Remember that your tester needn't even sit into your car if it isn't right. ▽ROTR **10 & 11**

The Six Point Check

There's a useful six-point check which you should carry out every time you sit in to drive:

1. **Door** – Make sure it's properly closed.
2. **Seat** – Adjust it properly so that you can hold the steering wheel easily and reach the foot pedals comfortably . . . knees slightly bent.
3. **Safety Belt** – You must wear it! Your tester does not have to wear a safety belt while conducting a test. ▽ROTR **11, 12 & 13**
4. **Mirrors** – Adjust the rear-view and wing mirrors for maximum view.
5. **Handbrake** – Make sure it's fully engaged.
6. **Gears** – Always ensure that you start up the engine in neutral. Check that the gear stick moves freely in neutral before starting up.

REMEMBER

> When you go for your Driving Test you will have to sign a declaration that your vehicle is in roadworthy condition.
> Make sure that it is!
> Don't allow your vehicle to fail your Test for you!

Controlling Your Vehicle

Getting out on the road successfully and staying there safely is a matter of feet, hands and head! You must maintain full control of your vehicle at all times, making proper use of the accelerator, footbrake, clutch and gears, handbrake and steering wheel. Wear comfortable shoes which won't slip off the foot pedals.

Feet First – The Foot Pedals

The **A, B, C** of driving refers to the foot pedals:

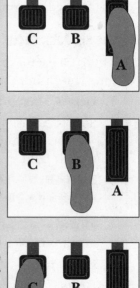

A is for the accelerator which you always press with the right foot. This is the pedal which controls the rate at which petrol/gas/diesel flows to the engine.

B is for the brake which you always press with the right foot. This is the pedal which is used for slowing and stopping the vehicle. It will take some practice before you learn to move your right foot smoothly from the accelerator to the brake and back again. Use the footbrake very little, if at all, when cornering. It is preferable, when cornering, to 'cover' the brake and only to apply pressure as necessary. Always operate the brake smoothly, except in an emergency.

C is for the clutch (pedal) which you press always and only with the left foot. This is the pedal which you use to engage and disengage the gears. The gears are for matching the power of the engine with the speed of the vehicle. Smoothness of operation is all important and it is not easy, at first, to find the 'biting point' where the clutch engages.

Clutch Control

You must only use the clutch for changing gears, or for disengaging the gears just before you stop. 'Coasting' with the clutch pedal down or rolling along in neutral are dangerous habits. They will be viewed seriously by your tester as you are not in control of your vehicle.

While driving, the best position for your left foot is flat on the floor, just to the left of the clutch pedal. Only raise your foot to the clutch pedal when you intend to change gear or stop. Resting your foot on the clutch pedal is known as 'riding the clutch' and can cause unnecessary wear on the clutch-plate.

When changing gears, don't press down on the clutch and accelerator together. Doing so will cause the engine to 'roar' and will waste petrol. When you are changing gears it's –
off the accelerator / on the clutch /
off the clutch / on the accelerator.

Automatics

If you drive a car which has automatic transmission, then you will have only two foot pedals – an accelerator and a brake. Use your right foot for these pedals and always ensure the brakes are in good order.

The gear-shift system is very straightforward:

P is for PARK, which disengages the gears and 'locks' the transmission.

R is for REVERSE.

N is for NEUTRAL, which disengages the gears. It may be used when stopped temporarily in traffic. The handbrake should be applied when in neutral. Automatic engines will start-up only in either NEUTRAL or PARK.

D is for DRIVE, which allows standard forward movement.

2 is for negotiating reasonably steep inclines up or down.

1 is for very steep inclines.

L or LOW is an alternative in some automatics for the 2 and 1 gears. It is for negotiating inclines.

Automatic vehicles have a special 'kick-down' facility which will give quick acceleration. This may be used when overtaking. The accelerator is pushed hard to the floor and the gears will drop back and allow for a quick build-up of speed.

The Gears

When none of the gears are engaged, your vehicle is in NEUTRAL. Your vehicle should always be in neutral when: you start up the engine; you re-start the engine if your vehicle cuts out in traffic; if you expect a long delay in traffic; or when you have stopped to park on level ground.

Choosing the Correct Gear for Starting, Stopping and Slowing

First Gear is generally used for moving off or for moving very slowly (speeds 0 – 10mph approx.). If you have been moving slowly in first gear and find you have to stop, then stop in that gear, but you don't have to change down from second to first gear to stop.

Second Gear is for building speed, for going up and down steep inclines, for turning corners and sharp bends and for stopping (speeds up to 30mph (48km/h) approx.). You may start off in second gear if you are moving off down a steep incline. It is not essential to change down to second gear for stopping, but it will help to slow your vehicle.

Third Gear is for building up speed and it may also be used as you slow down or stop (speeds up to a maximum of 50mph (80km/h) approx.). It is generally used approaching traffic lights, pedestrian crossings, roundabouts, junctions or when approaching an obvious hazard. Third gear is suitable for negotiating wide bends.

Fourth Gear is for travelling at speed. It is not usually used when you are stopping, but it may be, especially for an emergency stop.

Fifth Gear is a feature of many modern vehicles. It is used for cruising at speed. You're unlikely to need it while on test, but it may be appropriate to use it if you are required to drive on an open stretch of road. Not every car will have a fifth gear.

Reverse Gear is used for reversing! Careful and competent reversing is essential if you want to pass your test. It demands considerable practice.

Changing gear smoothly also takes practice. You must learn to choose the correct gear for each situation. Too high a gear at slow speed will labour or even stall the engine. Too low a gear at high speed will cause the engine to roar. Smooth gear-changing involves moving your left hand and left foot together and listening to the engine. Become accustomed to the sounds it makes. With the clutch pedal down, the gear is not engaged. Your vehicle is just rolling along and you are not in control. Stay away from the clutch unless you are changing gear or you are just about to stop.

The Brakes

The footbrake, which you always press with your right foot, is for slowing and stopping your vehicle. When you are stopping you use both feet, but you do not use them at exactly the same time. The order is very important. Always use the brake first and you then use the clutch. As you press the footbrake and your vehicle comes to a halt, you must press the clutch down fully so that the engine won't stall and cut out. If the engine does cut out, apply the handbrake and choose neutral before starting up again. So when stopping, the rule is: press the brake first and then the clutch.

The Handbrake

The handbrake is an essential part of your braking system. Make sure it's fully on when you are starting the engine and when you are stopped or parked on level ground. Apply it when you have stopped in traffic or when you are stopped or parked on any incline. You may need to use it during the Turnabout, where your vehicle is likely to roll forward or backwards.

Generally your gear lever will be in the neutral position when you have the handbrake on but not, of course, when you are about to move off. When you are engaging the handbrake always do so smoothly, pressing the button and holding it in to avoid wear on the ratchet.

When disengaging the handbrake, always make sure to let it down all the way. Many vehicles have a red light on the instrument panel which shows when the handbrake is engaged. Watch out for this! Should you forget to release the handbrake when moving off, the engine may stall and cut out. This is a fairly common error among learner drivers, so try to avoid it.

The handbrake on most cars operates only on the rear brakes, so, in order to avoid causing a skid, never use the handbrake to stop your car, unless it's an absolute emergency! In automatic cars the handbrake suppresses the drive system and should always be used when stopped in traffic, in the Drive position, for any length of time.

The Steering Wheel & Steering

When it comes to directing your vehicle, hold the steering wheel firmly in both hands so that you can move it easily and comfortably.

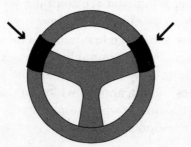

Hold it here in the 10 to 2 or quarter to 3 position.

You should hold the steering wheel with both hands, but when you are changing gears this will not be possible. Modern vehicles have fingertip controls for the indicators, windscreen wipers and horn. This means that you don't have to let the steering wheel go to operate them. If you do have to take your hand off the steering wheel to operate a signal or change gear, return it to the correct position immediately afterwards.

When turning the wheel, always feed it between your fingers. Maintain contact with the rim while pushing up and pulling down, as required, to manoeuvre right or left. Your hands should not cross over each other. Nor should you let the wheel slip through your fingers – always feed it!

Make sure to keep both hands firmly on the wheel when you are stopping and when you are stopped in traffic. Don't be tempted to leave your left hand resting on the gear-shift or to rest your right elbow on the door. If your vehicle has power-assisted steering you will find it particularly easy to manoeuvre in a restricted area. Avoid over-steering on (or after) cornering.

Never allow the steering wheel to slip from your grasp after a turn or manoeuvre. Always hold the wheel with both hands when stopping. Don't over-steer on (or after) cornering.

Signalling

When you are motoring you must let other road users know what you intend to do. Do this by signalling your intention clearly and in good time. Most of the time you will use your indicators to warn others of your intention, but there may be times when a hand signal will also be necessary. We shall look at hand signals later. ▽ROTR 14, 15 & 16

Always signal your intention to move off, change lanes, overtake, negotiate roundabouts, turn left or right, slow down, or pull in at the side of the road. Make sure to cancel your signal when you have completed your manoeuvre. Don't give contradictory signals, because these are potentially dangerous signals. Remember that signalling does not give you right of way!

Be aware that other road users may not see or understand your signal. When you observe the signals of other road users, you cannot assume that they mean what you think they mean, particularly when another motorist flashes headlights at you. Some road users don't signal at all. Pay attention and try to read their minds.

Should another motorist beckon you, always be extremely cautious. If you choose to act on their signal, the responsibility is yours. Never take it for granted that their signal can be relied upon.

Brake Lights

Brake lights can provide useful clues about the intentions of drivers in front of you, but be aware that the brake lights on the vehicle in front may not be working. Your brake lights can prove helpful to motorists following you. Always signal your intention clearly and in good time.

The Horn

The horn is a warning signal. Over-use or aggressive use of the horn can lead to test faults. But if you do not use it when you should, you can also incur test faults. Also, take into account that another road user who is deaf, or indeed using a personal stereo, may not hear your horn. Helpful use of the horn will indicate to other road users that there is danger about. Except in an emergency, you should not sound the horn between 11.30 at night and 7 o'clock in the morning.

Always signal your intention clearly and in good time!
Signalling does not confer Right of Way.
Conflicting signals can be confusing for other road users.
Never take it for granted that others' signals can be relied on!
You must know and be able to demonstrate hand signals!

Part 3: On the Road

Using Your Head – C.O.A.P.

Your Tester is trained in observation and is going to be checking that you are too! There are several key elements which you must learn and apply: **Concentration, Observation, Anticipation** and **Patience** are essential in safe driving.

Concentration involves self-discipline. You cannot allow your attention to wander. Nowadays, traffic conditions are often hectic and you need a clear head and a clear view through your windscreens as you observe and anticipate what lies ahead.

Observation involves knowing what is going on around you at all times. There are four areas which you must monitor constantly: the **far** distance, the **middle** distance, the area **near** you and you must also know what is happening to your **rear**.

Areas to Monitor

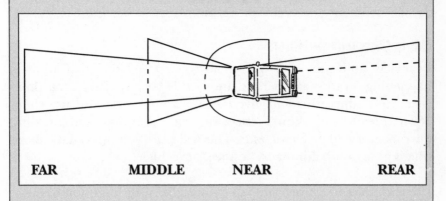

| FAR | MIDDLE | NEAR | REAR |

25

Anticipation: As you are motoring, your brain registers an enormous amount of information. Your safety and the safety of other road users depends on how you process that information. When you **observe** a particular situation, you must **think** about what is to be done. **Decide** on what *you* intend to do and then **act wisely** on your decision. You must watch out for other road users, especially pedestrians. They may not be concentrating, so *you* must. Observe the rules of the road *and* also observe the behaviour of others. Anticipate their actions in order to stay one step ahead of danger. Be patient with, and make allowances for, other road users!

Patience is a virtue all sensible motorists aspire to. Remember that you are not in competition with other road users. Drive defensively rather than aggressively. It is not up to you to force others to behave sensibly. Make allowances for the motoring failures of others and give others a chance. If you are a risk taker you could be an accident maker!

```
C  –  CONCENTRATE
O  –  OBSERVE
A  –  ANTICIPATE
P  –  PATIENCE!
```

Aids to Observation – Mirrors

Rear-view and wing mirrors allow you to see some of what is happening on the road behind and beside your vehicle. Keep them clean and adjust them to give you maximum view and use them often. Ideally you should check in your rear-view and/or wing mirrors every 20 or 25 seconds. This will keep you up to date about what's going on behind and beside your vehicle.

Use your mirrors before and after you signal your intention to move off, change lanes, turn left or right, overtake parked or moving vehicles, carry out any manoeuvre, slow down or pull in to stop. Check in your mirror after you have completed a manoeuvre too.

So the drill is: **Mirror/Signal/Mirror/Manoeuvre.**

Practise looking in your mirrors while your vehicle is stationary. Learn the difference between what you *see* in your mirror and what is *actually* happening. If your mirrors are flat, you will see less. If they are curved convexly, you will see more, but distances will be distorted. Learn to assess the speed and distance of vehicles coming up behind you. Be aware that many motorists, even though they shouldn't, will accelerate to avoid letting you out ahead of them. Allow for this!

Some drivers can adjust their wing mirrors from inside their vehicle. This can help with your reversing manoeuvre. But re-adjust the mirror *after* you have completed the manoeuvre. *Never* adjust them while on the move.

Hindrances to Observation – Blindspots

Blindspots are the parts of the road which, for one reason or another, cannot be seen from your vehicle. Note that the closer you are to an object, the more it blocks your view. This is especially true when travelling close behind another vehicle. Your roof supports and even your rear-view mirror can obstruct your view to the front. Pedestrians, cyclists and motorcyclists all present a narrow profile. You must be especially watchful for them. If in doubt, particularly at junctions, you may lean forward and look around the roof supports or under the rear-view mirror. Use your mirrors very often. Your tester will be ideally positioned to see if you are using your mirrors. You must also take account of your own blindspots and those of other road users. Keep your windscreens free from obstruction. Stickers, badges, cushions, dangly toys and even your L-plates are potential obstructions.

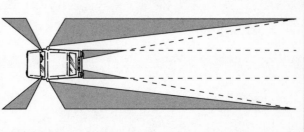

Grey areas indicate the blindspots which may affect your view from the driver's seat. The rear-view mirror itself may also impair your view to the front

Hazards

A hazard is any dangerous or potentially dangerous situation for you or for others. There are many things to consider, e.g. how you are feeling; the condition of your vehicle; other road users; the time of day; the environment in which you are driving; the route you are taking; weather and lighting conditions (if there's a glare you may need sunglasses); the road surface, particularly where there are potholes, and if you are near roadworks. Gravel and fallen leaves can build up at the roadside, especially on bends. Be very cautious if you encounter these.

The weather has an enormous bearing on driving conditions too. If rain falls after a long dry spell, roads can be greasy and dangerous. During heavy rain and snow, visibility may be considerably reduced. Some motorists and other road users act selfishly in poor weather conditions and may take unnecessary risks in a bid to get to their destination quickly. You can fail the test for not recognising hazards and dealing appropriately with them. For example – *always* give adequate clearance when overtaking cyclists especially.

Keep Your Distance – The Two Second Rule

You must continually anticipate what the driver in the vehicle ahead of you may do. Never drive too close to the vehicle in front of you. Stay really well back when road or weather conditions are bad. 'The Two Second Rule' may be used to gauge the correct distance between your vehicle and the vehicle in front. Pick a point of reference, e.g. a road sign or light pole. When the vehicle in front draws level with your chosen landmark, say to yourself: *"Only a fool breaks the two second rule!"*

It takes approximately two seconds to say this. Your vehicle should not reach the 'landmark' until you have finished saying the phrase, thus ensuring a safe gap in ideal road conditions. This will prove impractical when motoring about town, but it is very useful when you're on the open road. Avoid 'tailgating'. It is very dangerous.

 37 & 38

Expecting the Unexpected

Try to expect the unexpected and avoid being taken by surprise. By doing so, you may be able to prevent hazards arising or take evasive action if they do. Be careful not to pose a hazard for other road users. Ideally *your* driving should not force another to change course, slow down or stop.

Any change of position on the road is a manoeuvre, so:
1. MIRROR   2. SIGNAL   3. MIRROR   4. MANOEUVRE or M/S/M/M.

Courtesy vs. Road Rage

A discourteous driver is a potentially dangerous driver and during your test you will be required to show *proper regard for the safety and convenience of other road users*. Courtesy on the road costs nothing but it pays dividends. Don't be antagonistic towards other road users. Remember that *road rage* is a choice! Show restraint, stay calm, act wisely and be responsible instead!

Other Road Users

Pedestrians

Pedestrians of all ages are unpredictable. Children are especially so. Those who jaywalk may want to make you angry. Groups of children, as well as teenage and adult pedestrians may behave belligerently. Drivers must give way to pedestrians *at all times* and must never place even antagonistic pedestrians at risk. Pedestrians often don't seem to realise the danger they pose. It may well be true to say that common sense is not common!

Be especially careful if your test is being carried out near a school or a playground, or in a built-up area where there are children playing, or during rush-hour. Children who play in the street become blasé about the dangers of being near traffic. If you see a ball rolling onto the road, *don't* be tempted to keep your eye on the ball. Watch instead for the child who may be following it and react correctly to the hazard they may pose. This may involve sounding the horn, slowing down or stopping, or all of these.

Note how pedestrians who are crossing a busy road may make a dash towards the centre of the roadway and stop. Then when the opportunity arises they make for the other pavement – but observe how they *slow down* as they reach it! Pedestrians running for or alighting from buses often risk crossing the road without taking proper observation. Show particular consideration for elderly people and those who are infirm.

A pedestrian with a buggy or pram may turn off the pavement suddenly. They may push the buggy into the path of oncoming traffic. Be prepared for this and act accordingly. Look *under* the wheels of parked vehicles, so you can see the feet of pedestrians who are not tall enough to be seen otherwise. Give way to pedestrians at crossings and pedestrian lights. If pedestrians are already crossing the road or crossing at a junction where you intend to turn, *they have right of way!*

▽ 23, 49 & 50

Cyclists and Motorcyclists

Like pedestrians, these road users have a narrow profile and you may not see them easily, especially when you and they are moving. Allow that, even though they should, many do not look around or signal before they manoeuvre. This is often the case when they are turning left at a junction.

Observe how they overtake parked vehicles and how they tend to weave through traffic. Children on bicycles, especially groups cycling to and from school, are notoriously unpredictable. Be particularly considerate in bad weather and/or when you intend to overtake, turn left or right. Take great care opening the doors when you are parked. Avoid driving in cycle lanes. If you must cross them, e.g. when turning left, proceed with caution.

Animal Traffic

Persons in charge of animals have the right to signal you to slow down or stop. Never sound your horn in this situation. Show extra care and consideration in country areas where animal traffic is likely, and take particular notice of warning signs which relate to domestic and wild animals.

▽ 50

Reading the Road

Road signs and road markings will help you to *read the road* ahead of you. You must know what's going on around you at *all* times and you can practise the skill of reading the road even when you are not driving. When you are travelling as a front passenger, observe the far distance, the middle distance, what is near and occasionally glance over your shoulder to see what is to the rear, but remember that your viewpoint in the passenger seat is much *different* to that of the driver.

Fields of View

What you can see of the road ahead will depend on the local topography. In built-up areas, houses, buildings, walls, fences, hedges and hoardings may obscure your view. Other vehicles, whether moving or parked will also reduce your field of view, as will bends, hills or hollows in the road. The obscured area is often called 'dead ground'. It will be impossible to predict what hazards the unseen area may hide, so exercise extreme care!

Reading the Signs

You will encounter many different road signs and markings as you are motoring. You must understand all these signs because they're always *telling* you something. Be prepared to act according to the signs you see. It is particularly advisable to become familiar with all of the road signs and markings in the area where your driving test will be carried out.

Warning Signs advise you of hazards or potential hazards.   ▽ᴿᴼᵀᴿ 20, 66, 67 & 68

Regulatory Signs often indicate the direction traffic may or may not take. For the most part, these signs are mandatory and must be obeyed. Except for STOP and YIELD signs, regulatory signs are usually circular with a red ring, a white background and black arrow markings. Some regulatory signs have a white ring, a blue background and white arrow markings.

▽ᴿᴼᵀᴿ 17, 18, 19, 36 & 65

Information Signs advise you about distances and direction. They are generally rectangular or in the shape of an arrow. They may also appear as white painted signs on the road. Tourism information signs are generally coloured brown, but some are green.   ▽ᴿᴼᵀᴿ 20 & 68

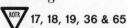

Eolas do Thurasoiri
TOURIST INFORMATION

Motorway Signs inform you of the beginning and end of motorway restrictions. Remember that L-drivers (and certain other road users, which you should know about) are denied access to motorways. 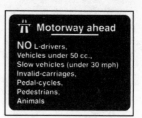 21 & 31

Road Markings are either white or yellow.

 18 & 30

Hatched Markings are white or yellow diagonal stripes. They are to be found in areas where streams of traffic must be separated. They may also form a traffic island for right-turning traffic.

The rule for hatched markings which divide traffic streams is that if the markings are edged with a broken white line on your side you may cross *only* after you have signalled your intention and *if it is safe to do so*. If it is edged with a solid white line you may not cross. As you approach a right-hand turn, following traffic may not overtake you if this means driving over the hatched area. ▽ 30

Other Road Markings and Roadwork Signs may consist of an inverted white triangle, which means YIELD, or yellow zig-zag markings near schools with the legend – SCHOOL KEEP CLEAR. Roadwork signs are warning signs specific to roadworks. Temporary traffic lights and/or semaphore flags may be used also. These must be obeyed. ▽ 22 & 68

Starting Up

When you start your engine *always* ensure that the handbrake is on and that the gear shift is in neutral. *This also applies if you cut out in traffic.* If your car has a diesel engine with a 'glow light', you must wait until the light goes out before turning the ignition.

In cold weather you may need to use the *choke* to increase the fuel flow and reduce the amount of air which mixes with it. If your car has a manual choke don't forget to push the lever in again when the engine is warm. If you leave the choke out, the engine will run 'high' and waste fuel.

With the choke out, the vehicle may also seem to have a mind of its own, impeding you when you're trying to stop. Automatic chokes will self-adjust. Read the appropriate part of the owner's manual if you drive your own car.

Moving Off

Many learner drivers have difficulty learning to move off smoothly. The problem usually lies with lack of clutch control. Moving off involves achieving a balance between the use of the accelerator and clutch pedals. You obviously cannot look at your feet when you're driving, so you must *listen* instead for the engine revs. You will also learn to *feel* the biting point as the clutch engages first gear.

Let's see how it might go . . .
- Start the engine in neutral, handbrake on.
- Press the clutch down fully and choose first gear.
- Check in your mirror to see if it's safe to move off.
- Signal right to indicate your intention.
- As you release the clutch pedal to engage first gear, hold the accelerator down a little.
- Listen and you'll hear the sound of the engine die down a little and you'll feel the gear engaging, trying to pull the car forward (the biting point).
- Release the handbrake and then, *if it is safe to move,* release the clutch fully as you press down smoothly on the accelerator.
- Check in your mirror again before moving off.
- It's important to look over your right shoulder as you move off.
- Once in the stream of traffic, check your mirror and cancel your signal.

The added precaution of looking over the right shoulder is a very important one. It overcomes the 'blindspot' and any distortion caused by the mirrors. Never take unnecessary risks – *always* look!

Any change of position on the road is a manoeuvre, so:
1. MIRROR   2. SIGNAL   3. MIRROR
4. LOOK OVER SHOULDER   5. MANOEUVRE

Moving Off at an Angle

If you are parked behind another vehicle, then you will have to move off from the kerb at an angle. You must move off safely, giving enough clearance from the vehicle in front. Clutch control is crucial here and so is observation. Make allowances for any traffic coming towards you as well as traffic coming up behind you. Remember that if the vehicle in front of you is large and you are close to it, the more danger there will be as you try to move out into the stream of traffic. You may need to reverse a little before you have enough room to move away. Be very careful! While all of this may seem very straightforward, you can expect to stall many times before you get it right.

Gathering Speed

To build up speed you should move up through the gears smoothly. Don't forget to keep your foot *off* the clutch between gear changes.

Road Position and Lane Discipline

You may be on the road, but *where* on the road are you? You must position your vehicle correctly on the road and your tester will be watching to see just how well positioned you are on straight roads, on bends and corners. Keep in the proper lane and keep within lane markings. If the lanes are not marked, then you must imagine them and drive as though they were there. Make sensible use of available road space.

In city driving you may find that the left lane is almost totally free of traffic. This is because many motorists fail to read the road and simply follow blindly behind the vehicle in front. Keep your distance from the vehicle in front of you.

Driving on the left means staying left of the centre line if there is only one lane. A good rule of thumb is to keep an eye on the shore gratings at the side of the road. Keep a little to the right of them and you'll be in the correct position.

If there are two or three lanes, then stay in the left lane. Use the outer lane for overtaking or if you intend to turn right. The same rule applies if there are one, two or three lanes: KEEP LEFT, PASS RIGHT!

If there are four lanes, then watch out for filter lanes to the left and right and position your vehicle accordingly. ▽ROTR 23 & 24

Filter Lanes

If there is a left filter lane and you're in it, then you'll be obliged to follow the white arrow road markings and go left. So, if you intend to go straight ahead, move into the lane which is second from the left. ▽ROTR 23, 24 & 26

Dual Carriageways

Keep in the left lane unless you intend to overtake or turn right and have signalled your intention. A dual carriageway is not like a motorway, as other vehicles have limited access and there are speed restrictions. Crossing or turning onto a dual carriageway demands great care, concentration and observation. 28 & 29

Motorways

Learner drivers may not drive on motorways, but must know all the rules and signs which apply to them. 31, 32 & 33

Right of Way/Priority

When you are moving off, changing lanes, overtaking, approaching a junction or roundabout, turning left or right, slowing or stopping, you must Give Way to other road users.

Also Give Way to Garda, Ambulance and Fire Brigade vehicles if they display blue flashing lights and/or sound their sirens. 36 & 37

As a learner driver you are prohibited from driving on motorways.
When you pass your test you should arrange some
Motorway Driving Lessons with your instructor.

Changing Lanes

Whether you are moving into a lane to your right or to your left, changing lanes involves the M/S/M/M routine and giving way as appropriate. A *very* quick glance over your shoulder and/or careful use of the wing mirrors will ensure that it's safe to manoeuvre. Do not change lanes unless you have to.

Overtaking

Now you know how to keep your place, but suppose you want to change that place, say, with the vehicle in front of you? If you want to overtake, you must check the vehicle in front of you and indicate your intention to those behind you. You'll need a clear view of the road ahead – remember what was said before about proximity to the vehicle in front reducing your view. Stay well back so you can get a good view of the road ahead. Make good use of your mirrors.

- Use the M/S/M/M routine again. Check that *you* are not being overtaken.
- Indicate *clearly and in good time.*
- When you have a clear view of the road ahead, move out smoothly and move on smartly. Do not stay within the other driver's blindspot any longer than necessary.
- When you have overtaken, do *not* cut in.
- When you can see what you've overtaken in your rear-view mirror, then it's safe to move back in to the left again. You may indicate as you do so and check your mirror again.

Where You May Not Overtake

There are many places where it's simply *not* safe to overtake, for example on a corner or a bend. At the brow of a hill or at a hump-backed bridge your view will be obscured by the 'dead ground' in the hollows (c.f. Fields of View). It may be *illegal*, as well as dangerous, to overtake, e.g. at traffic lights, over a continuous white line, or within the zig-zags at crossings.

Overtaking on the Left

The motto KEEP LEFT, PASS RIGHT generally applies to overtaking but there *are* times when you *may* overtake on the left. Check these out in your Rules of the Road as they are commonly asked in the oral part of the Test. ▼ 25

Safety First

When you are overtaking or being overtaken, you should always THINK SAFETY and ACT SAFELY. Avoid causing danger or inconvenience to other road users. When you are being overtaken, *never* accelerate. Allow the other vehicle to overtake you. Slow down if necessary.

Progress and Speed

Learning to judge the appropriate speed for moving off, driving on the straight, negotiating corners and bends will take time and practice. You will be expected to keep up with the traffic flow (keeping within the speed limit).

You should not stop unless you have to. This applies as you are entering a roundabout, approaching a YIELD sign, turning left or right. You must not cause an obstruction, especially at junctions. Busy junctions and traffic lights are notoriously difficult for learner drivers as many road users refuse to show them any consideration.

You must be able to stop *within* the distance you can see to be clear, but at the same time you must not drive so cautiously that you cause danger to or obstruct other drivers. You can actually fail the Test for not making proper progress. In a 40mph (64km/h) area you should drive *at* that speed, *if it is safe to do so!*

Speed Limits

When you're out on the road you *must* obey the speed limit. In built-up areas this means *not* exceeding 30mph (48km/h). Outside the speed limit area motorists are currently bound by a maximum speed of 60mph (96km/h). The maximum speed allowed on motorways is 70mph (112km/h). Heavy Goods vehicles are limited to a maximum speed of 50mph (80km/h).   ▽ROTR 37 & 38

Position, Speed and Observation

You know the footwork which will keep you going smoothly and safely. You know how to keep things properly in hand. You know how to use your head to **Concentrate**, **Observe** (think, decide) and **Anticipate** (act wisely) as well as staying **Patient**. You now about checking **far** distance, **middle** distance, **near** and **rear**. You know how to keep and how to change your place. You know how to adopt the correct **position** on the road; adjust your **speed** to the intended manoeuvre and **observe** carefully.

Junctions and Intersections

'It's a rare road that has no turning,' the old saying goes and junctions and intersections have signs *and* rules which apply specifically to them.

Roads of Equal Importance

These signs mean that you are approaching roads of equal importance, and priority is given to traffic coming from the *right!* If you intend to go straight ahead then:

- Assume the correct **position**, keeping in the left lane.
- Check in your mirror and adjust your **speed**.
- Change gear if you have to.
- **Observe** carefully – keeping a sharp eye on the junction as you come to it and check right and left as you go through.
- Give way, as necessary, to traffic coming from your right.

Major Roads to Minor Roads

When passing a minor road you have priority or right of way. Although you have the right to proceed, there's no point in being dead right! In rural areas watch out for farm traffic crossing from one minor road to another. In urban areas watch out especially for cyclists. Only proceed *if it's safe to do so*!

Minor Roads to Major Roads – Giving Way

When you see any of the minor to major road warning signs you may see either a YIELD RIGHT OF WAY sign, STOP sign (or TRAFFIC LIGHTS sign). You'll probably find a white STOP line across your side of the junction too! YIELD and STOP signs show that traffic on the road you wish to enter has *priority* over you. Where there is a YIELD sign and you intend to turn left, you must give way to traffic coming from the right. If you intend to turn right, give way to traffic coming from either direction, i.e. slow down or stop.

When you approach a STOP sign, you *must* stop at the sign or the line, *even if* the road you wish to enter is clear. Give way to traffic as necessary. You will fail your test if you 'dribble through' at a STOP sign. If you intend to turn left, you will increase your view of the road you wish to enter by stopping well to the left at the stop line. ᴿᴼᵀᴿ 36 & 37

Always heed regulatory signs painted on the roadway, e.g. NO ENTRY sign and BUS LANE sign. ᴿᴼᵀᴿ 19 & 35

Traffic Lights

Approaching a junction, you may see a TRAFFIC
LIGHTS AHEAD sign, so be prepared to stop at that
junction. Traffic lights *must* be obeyed.

RED means STOP behind the line.
AMBER means STOP behind the line – *unless it's unsafe to do so.*
AMBER does not mean race the lights!
GREEN means GO – but *only if it's safe to do so!* 26

Move into the correct lane at traffic lights, especially where there are
filter lights. As filter lights *must* be obeyed, you don't want to end up
having to turn left after you have been told by your examiner to go
straight ahead. Expect green traffic lights to change against you.
Drive at a speed which will enable you to stop before the line.

 19 & 26

Pedestrian Lights

Pedestrian lights near junction lights may be linked and may change
against you, even if there is no pedestrian preparing to cross. Be
ready for this! Pedestrian lights on a filter lane may have a flashing
amber arrow instead of a green light. Only proceed *if it's safe to do so!*

If traffic lights are broken proceed as if they were RED and be on the
lookout for a Garda on traffic duty. 55 & 56

Many car drivers believe that it is necessary to swing
to the right before making a left-hand turn and to swing
to the left before making a right-hand turn. This is not so!
This potentially dangerous practice should be avoided.
It also shows a lack of knowledge which could well
ensure that you fail your Driving Test.

Turning Left

Remember the M/S/M/M routine and the **Position, Speed** and **Observation** drill.

- Position yourself correctly in the left lane.
- Check your MIRROR and SIGNAL your intention clearly and in good time. If you have been told to take the *second* turning on the left *don't* signal until you have passed the centre of the first left turn. Signalling too soon could confuse other road users as to your intention.
- As a general rule you should take a left-hand turn in second gear.
- Having changed down to second, ease off the accelerator and cover the brake with your right foot, pressing gently, if you need to. It is *very* important *not* to accelerate into a corner or to brake heavily on a corner.
- Don't swing too wide on the corner.
- Keep reasonably close to the kerb.
- Check in your MIRROR again, allowing for any cyclists or motorcyclists who might have come up on your left, between your car and the kerb.
- Observe left and right *on* the turn.
- Don't mount or bump the kerb.
- GIVE WAY, as necessary, to pedestrians who have begun to cross.
- MANOEUVRE smartly, and maintain reasonable progress.
- Keep in the left lane.
- Check in your MIRROR again when you've straightened up after the turn.
- Don't change up through the gears until then.
- Remember *not* to let the steering wheel slip.
- Check to see that your signal is cancelled.

> If you are told to take the second turn on the left, then you must wait until you have passed the centre of the first turning before signalling your intention. Don't signal too early as this might confuse other motorists.

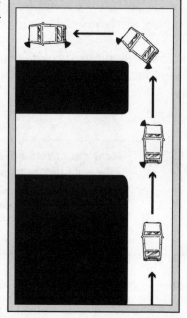

28

Turning Right

You will most likely be in the left-hand lane, so you'll have to change lanes. Use the M/S/M/M routine and the **Position, Speed** and **Observation** drill as well.

- Check your mirror and signal your intention *clearly and in good time.*
- Check the mirror once more before you manoeuvre.
- Move carefully into a position, just left of the centre line. As you change lanes, a *very* quick glance over your right shoulder may prove useful.
- Now you're in the correct POSITION for turning.
- Leave your signal flashing and adjust your SPEED by slowing down.
- GIVE WAY to those coming towards you, whether they are coming through the junction or turning left.
- If you don't have to stop, then be in second gear as you take the turn.
- If you *do* have to stop, take possession of the centre of the junction.
- Select first gear and hold the clutch down. Apply the handbrake, ready to move when the opportunity arises for you to complete the manoeuvre.
- Check to the front and use your mirror once more before you turn. Make sure to move round the centre of the junction. *Never cut the corner!*
- Move directly into the left lane and check in your mirror again.
- Don't let the steering wheel slip and check that your signal is cancelled.
- Whether you have taken the corner in first or second gear *don't* change up to the next gear until you have straightened up. 27 & 28

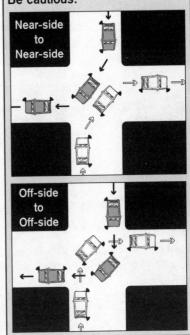

If you are told to turn right, then move from the left lane to a position just left of the centre-line. Hold your position until it is safe to complete the turn. You must choose the best way to negotiate the junction. Be cautious.

Near-side to Near-side

Off-side to Off-side

When you intend to turn right and someone coming against you wants to turn right also, you have two choices. You may pass near-side to near-side or pass off-side to off-side. Either method is acceptable, provided you manoeuvre safely. It is important to note that 'near-side' means the side nearest the kerb and that the 'off-side' means the driver's side.

If you choose the off-side to off-side turn, you must pass *behind* the other vehicle to make your turn. This method is preferrable, as your view is less restricted. If, however, the other vehicle is large, e.g. a bus or HGV you should choose the near-side to near-side method. Be very cautious because you have *added* blindspots. Sometimes the on-coming driver will not co-operate with you. This can be unnerving but you must make sure to clear the junction as soon as possible, especially if the lights turn red. At some junctions, the road markings *make* you turn right, in front of another vehicle. Obey these markings! Filter traffic lights must also be obeyed, so ensure that you're in the correct lane!

Yellow-Box Junctions

Junctions are like arteries. The last thing they need is a clot! So don't block the junction! This applies especially to yellow-box junctions. The yellow box is telling you 'Don't come in unless you can get out!' Never enter the box unless your exit road is clear! ◤ROTR 30

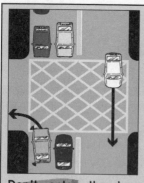 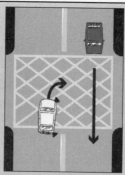 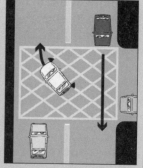

Don't enter the box unless your exit road is clear.	If you are turning right you may enter the box and wait until your path is clear.	However, even if you are turning right, don't enter the box and stop, if this obstructs traffic which has the right of way.

One-Way Systems

If you enter a one-way street and you're told to go right at the end, make sure to get into the right-hand lane in good time! Watch out for the signs indicating that you are returning to a TWO-WAY traffic system. Also look out for the NO ENTRY signs on a pole and marked on the roadway. 35

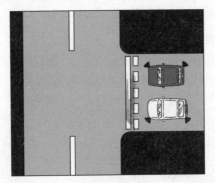

No Entry

Turn Left

Flow and Contra-Flow Bus Lanes

Make a mental note of the type of bus lane you are approaching. Check the times when restrictions apply. These are marked on a plate below the sign. You may drive in bus lanes at times other than those specified. 19 & 35

Bus Lane

Contra-flow Bus Lane

Roundabouts

Negotiating roundabouts can be very confusing at first, so let's see how you might deal with them.

As traffic volume is increasing, some roundabouts are regulated by traffic lights. In this case the rules for roundabouts AND traffic signals apply.

Turning Left at a Roundabout

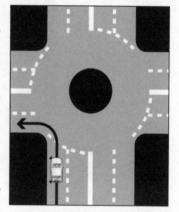

- POSITION? Stay in the left lane.
- Check in your MIRROR and SIGNAL left clearly and in good time.
- SPEED? Slow down, changing gear as necessary.
- OBSERVATION? Look right, left and right again.
- GIVE WAY, as necessary, to traffic on the roundabout.
- Check in your MIRROR again and MANOEUVRE.
- Keep in the left lane and move left off the roundabout.

Going Straight Ahead at a Roundabout

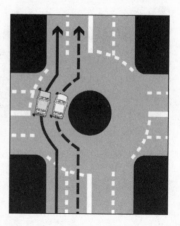

- POSITION? Stay in the left lane.
- Check your MIRROR.
- SPEED? Slow down, changing gear as necessary.
- OBSERVATION? Look right, left and right again entering the roundabout and give way, as you would if you were turning left.
- Don't signal until you have passed the centre of the first exit.
- Check in your MIRROR again and SIGNAL left.
- Stay in the left lane and leave the roundabout.
- Don't forget to use your MIRROR again as you straighten up.

Rules of the Road Quiz

The Rules of the Road Booklet

Remember the old adage:

> "When all else fails – read the instructions!"

So you will need a copy of the *Rules of the Road* as you prepare for your driving test. Study it well. You *must* become thoroughly familiar with its contents – even those sections which don't *seem* to apply directly to your driving test. Learn appropriate phrases and paragraphs off by heart and *always* put the rules into effect when you are on the road. The oral test usually consists of five or six questions. This may vary. Try yourself out now on this Quiz.

1. What do the following road warning signs mean?

2. What is the sequence of lights for motorists at a pelican crossing?

3. For whom should you stop?

4. Where may you not park?

5. What does a broken yellow line road marking mean?

6. What signs mean no entry?

7. When should you dip your headlights?

8. What should you do first in the event of an accident?

9. What do the zig-zag markings mean?

10. When may you cross a continuous white line?

11. Explain the meaning of a broken white line near the edge of the road.

12. When may you overtake on the left?

13. When may you overtake on the right?

14. At a controlled junction, to whom would you give way?

15. What does a flashing amber traffic light mean?

16. What does a green traffic light signify?

17. How must you enter a roundabout?

18. What does a clearway sign indicate?

19. What do the following regulatory signs mean?

The correct answers to questions **1-19** are on pages 74-76.

20. Road signs and markings give the road user vital clues about what lies ahead. You must be able to identify what type of sign each one is, and be aware of where it may occur. It is important to know which signs and markings go together and what you may be expected to do when you encounter them. Give the meaning of each of the following. Get someone to pick several at random for you to explain.

Find out what text appears on the signs below.

Combinations of the signs below may appear near roadworks. They are portable and much larger than usual signs.

🖩 Motorway ahead

NO.....................?
.....................?
.....................?
.....................?
.....................?
.....................?
.....................?

No 'what' on motorways?

Familiarise yourself with the road markings associated with the various road signs and the combination of signs.

Traffic Signs

The following pages show all the traffic signs you will need to know to pass your test.

Regulatory Signs

These signs often indicate the direction traffic may or may not take. For the most part, these signs are mandatory and must be obeyed.

Stop Sign	Yield Right of Way	Géill Slí	School Wardens Sign	No Left Turn
No Entry	No Right Turn	No Parking	Keep Left	Turn Left
Turn Right	Straight Ahead Only	Parking Permitted	Speed Limit	End of Speed Limit
Clearway – stopping or parking prohibited during times shown	Pedestrianised Street. Traffic Prohibited	Taxi Rank	Weight Restriction	

Warning Signs

These signs advise you of hazards or potential hazards.

Dangerous
Corner
Ahead

Dangerous Bend
Ahead

Series of
Dangerous
Corners Ahead

Series of
Dangerous
Bends Ahead

Junction ahead with roads of less importance
(the latter being indicated by arms of lesser width)

Junction ahead with road or roads of equal importance

Staggered
junction ahead
with roads of
less importance

Advance Warning of a major road (or dual carriageway)
ahead marked by a 'Stop' sign or 'Yield Right of Way' sign

Roundabout
Ahead

Traffic Lights
Ahead

Two-Way Traffic

Road Narrows
Dangerously
Ahead or Narrow
Bridge Ahead

Road Works
Ahead

Warnings Signs for Schools and Children

Sharp
Depression
Ahead

Series of Bumps
or Hollows
Ahead

Sharp Rise Ahead
e.g. Hump-Back
Bridge

Possible presence
of riders on
horseback ahead

Unprotected
Quay, Canal or
River Ahead

Slippery Stretch
of Road Ahead

Steep Ascent
Ahead

Steep Descent
Ahead

Low Bridge Ahead (a metric equivalent of the height limitations may be shown)

Level Crossing Ahead, unguarded by gates or lifting barriers

Level Crossing Ahead, guarded by gates or lifting barriers

Level Crossing ahead with lights and barriers

Roadwork Signs

These signs specific to roadworks must be obeyed.

Roadworks Ahead

Road Narrows Ahead at Left Hand Side

Traffic Cross-over Ahead

Traffic Lights Ahead

DIVERTED TRAFFIC →

MAJOR ROAD WORKS AHEAD

DETOUR 400m

Information Signs

These signs advise you about distances and direction.

Motorway Signs

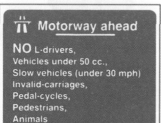

Motorway Ahead

Entry to Motorway

Approaching end
of motorway

Motorway Regulations
no longer apply

Turning Right at a Roundabout

- POSITION? Move into the right-hand lane approaching the roundabout.
- Well in advance of the roundabout you must MIRROR, SIGNAL, MIRROR and MANOEUVRE into the right-hand lane.
- SPEED? Slow down.
- GIVE WAY as necessary.
- OBSERVATION? Look right, left and right again.
- Leave your indicator on as you enter the roundabout.
- When you reach the centre of the exit *before* the one you intend to take, M/S/M/M into the left lane.
- Indicate that you intend turning left.
- Stay in the left lane and leave the roundabout.
- Check in your MIRROR again as you straighten up and build up speed.

There are single lane, double lane and three lane roundabouts. Choose the lane which suits your intended manoeuvre, but avoid cutting in on other traffic. If the left-hand lane is blocked as you approach the roundabout, choose the right-hand lane, but exercise extreme caution.

It may prove difficult to signal correctly when dealing with a mini traffic-calming roundabout. If there are any of these on your likely test route, then practise dealing with them until you can do so with confidence.

Accidents can occur at roundabouts when drivers fail to give way to those already on the roundabout. Allowances must be made for cyclists or motorcyclists when turning left. Pay particular attention to any vehicles stopped in front of you as you prepare to enter a roundabout. They may have to brake again before joining the flow of traffic.

ROTR 33 & 34

Always enter a roundabout by turning left.
Give way to traffic already on the roundabout.
Going left? Signal as you enter the roundabout.
Going straight ahead? Signal as you exit, but not as you enter.
Going right? Signal as you enter and again as you exit.

More About Stopping

Earlier we looked at the procedure for stopping – BRAKE first, then CLUTCH!

The same applies when you have to stop in traffic or if you're stopping to park. Normally, pulling in to the kerb goes like this:

- Check your MIRROR and SIGNAL your intention *clearly and in good time.*
- Change down to third gear or second gear, as necessary.
- Check in your MIRROR again, making allowances for cyclists or motorcyclists on the inside and stop reasonably close to the kerb.
- Brake first, then clutch, just before the engine stalls and cuts out.
- Apply the handbrake fully, change to neutral and stop the engine.

Stopping Distances

Stopping takes *time!* You must be able to stop *within the distance you can see to be clear.* Stopping distances are affected by the speed of your reaction (at least 1 second), your brakes and shock absorbers, the condition and air pressure of your tyres, the road surface and weather conditions, the size and weight of your vehicle and the speed at which you are travelling. Even at 30mph (48km/h) your reaction time and braking time will mean a total stopping distance of *at least* 26 yards (23 metres) and that's *only if* road conditions *and* the condition of your vehicle are ideal.

Keep your distance from the vehicle in front of you. Take account of all potential hazards. Stopping distances are drastically increased in poor weather conditions, but a vehicle ahead with anti-lock brakes may stop very quickly. When you encounter a hazard you may need to sound your horn to warn others of approaching danger. Keep this equation in mind:

Reaction Time	+	**Braking Time**	=	**Stopping Distance.**
1 second	+	5 seconds	=	26 yards at least (23 metres) at 30 mph (48 km/h)

 38 & 39

Emergency Stops

As a motorist you must ensure your own safety and the safety of other road users. Although an emergency stop is listed in the schedule of the driving test, it is not actually part of the test at present. However, you must know what to do if it becomes necessary. In an emergency stop you won't have time for the M/S/M/M routine. Your sole aim will be to stop and to do so safely, as quickly as possible and under control!

How to Stop in an Emergency

- Grip the steering-wheel *firmly* in *both* hands.
- Press *firmly* on the footbrake.
- When you must stop very quickly, pumping the brakes (cadence braking) can help prevent them from locking and help you avoid a skid.
- Stay well away from the clutch until the last moment.
- Then press it down fully, just before the engine stalls.
- When the vehicle is stopped, apply the handbrake and go into neutral.
- Before you move off again, check all around you and carry out the usual 'moving off' drill: MIRROR, SIGNAL, MIRROR, LOOK OVER THE RIGHT SHOULDER and then move off, *when it's safe to do so*.

Anti-Lock Brakes

Anti-lock brakes are a useful addition to any vehicle. But anti-lock brakes are only designed to increase your ability to stop safely. They cannot replace your observation, anticipation and safe driving skills. Read your motoring manual for details of the most effective use of this braking system. Remember that anti-lock brakes are less effective in poor road and weather conditions.

> When motoring behind another vehicle always keep your distance and remember that you must always be able to stop within the distance you can see to be clear!
> Practise 'The two-second rule'.

Skidding

A skid is caused when the tyres lose their grip on the road. You can avoid skidding by braking smoothly rather than harshly (especially on bends and corners); by ensuring that your tyres and brakes are in good condition; by allowing for the condition of the road (gravel, surface water, ice, snow, fallen leaves etc); by not braking and steering at the same time and by avoiding excessive acceleration in low gear.

The general rule for dealing with a skid is to stay away from the brake and ease off the accelerator. If your vehicle does skid, then turn the steering wheel in the same direction as the skid in order to bring the front and rear wheels into line with each other. You must also avoid over-compensating, otherwise you may start to skid in the other direction.

Bad driving, bad brakes, bad tyres and bad road and weather conditions and/or combinations of these can cause skidding.

Refer to your copy of the <u>Rules of the Road</u> pages 63 and 64 so that you know what to do in the event of an accident.

Part 4: Test Manoeuvres

Reversing

Two parts of the driving test which cause many learner drivers great stress are reversing and the turnabout. Yet, if you know the rules and practise the manoeuvres, you will have nothing to worry about. Reversing is all about good observation, good footwork, steering control and taking your time.

Your tester will ask you to pull in to the left and park at a spot convenient to a corner – e.g. *'Just beyond the next left turn!'*
- Use the MIRROR.
- Check for cyclists or motorcyclists coming up on your left.
- SIGNAL only when you have passed the centre of the left turn.
- Check the MIRROR again and park parallel to the kerb.
- Stop and put on the handbrake and go into neutral.

Now the tester will tell you to reverse. If it has been raining or your windscreens are obscured by condensation, why not wipe them? This is allowed and you want to give yourself the best advantage. (The windscreen heaters will stop them fogging up, but a little rub of washing up liquid on the inside before your test will help too!) You may leave your safety belt off during the reverse manoeuvre, but this is the *only* time during the test that you're allowed to do so.

Here is a suggested approach to this manoeuvre:
- Choose reverse gear smoothly. Keeping your right foot off the accelerator will keep it smooth and avoid that crunching sound in the gearbox.
- Look over your left shoulder out through the rear windscreen. Watch out for potential hazards – children playing or traffic coming up behind you.
- The rear-view mirror is not used in this manoeuvre, although the near-side wing mirror can prove useful during the reverse.

- Release the handbrake and ease up the clutch, putting little pressure, if any, on the accelerator.
- Watch where you have your hands. The usual position is changed to 5 past 7, right hand up and left down.
- Easing up and down on the clutch will help control your speed.
- When the rear wheels approach the corner, the kerb will seem to disappear under the left rear wheel.
- Now is the time to turn the steering wheel gently to the left.
- As you round the corner, the near-side rear wheel will move towards the kerb.
- On the apex of the turn, your right wing will be very exposed.
- You *must* look to the right at this point, as you are presenting a danger to traffic coming from the right. You *do not* have right of way, so it may be necessary to stop at this point to allow up-coming traffic to proceed.
- Don't straighten up too soon or you will end up too far out from the kerb.
- Straighten up by gently feeding the steering wheel to the right.
- When you see the kerb in the centre of the rear windscreen, you'll know you're properly aligned.

Some corners are wide, while others are sharp. You will need to get lots of practice negotiating both types. If you mount or bump the kerb you may fail the test. Constant repetition will improve your confidence and skill. Don't underestimate the need to be really competent at reversing both for your test and for afterwards.

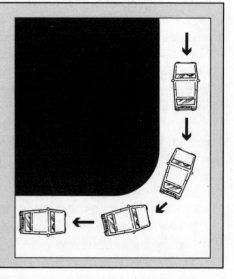

Keep reasonably close to the kerb and avoid swinging out too wide. Always yield to traffic coming from behind you. Don't mount or bump the kerb either. You will be expected to reverse for a reasonable distance after you have rounded the corner, before stopping.

You may find reversing confusing at first. Remember that when you are reversing, the rear of your car will go in the direction you steer. Left lock means the rear turns left, towards the kerb. Right lock means the rear turns right, away from the kerb. Your driving tester will probably open the door to see how far from the kerb you have stopped your vehicle. Before moving off again, you *must* put your safety belt on and carry out the usual M/S/M/M drill. Look over your right shoulder too. Practise reversing around both wide and sharp bends. You will *not* be asked to reverse from a minor to a major road. This is both illegal and dangerous.

> **Good observation is essential when reversing.**

Parking

Always park legally and safely, close to and parallel to the kerb. Never park more than 18in (45cm) out from the kerb. When your test is over, you will be expected to park your vehicle near the testing centre. You may be able to drive easily into a parking spot. However, it isn't always possible to drive into a parking spot. Reversing in usually works better. This is called oblique parking, which means that it is not straightforward. With practice you'll easily be able to judge if there's enough room for you to park in a particular spot. You must also know where not to park.

▽ROTR 45 – 48

> **Always signal your intention clearly and in good time!**
> **Signalling does not confer Right of Way.**
> **Conflicting signals can be confusing for other road users.**
> **Never take it for granted that others' signals can be relied on!**
> **You must know and be able to demonstrate hand signals!**

Reverse Parking

So let's see how you might approach this manoeuvre:

- Because you're pulling into the side, you must follow the M/S/M/M routine and stop parallel to the vehicle, behind which you intend to park.

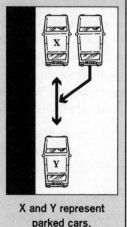

> The ability to reverse-park is essential. Ask your instructor to help you to perfect this manoeuvre before your test. Practise until you perfect it!

X and Y represent parked cars.

- Apply the handbrake.
- Release your safety belt, if you wish.
- Choose REVERSE GEAR and, releasing the handbrake, look over your left shoulder as you reverse *slowly* and *carefully*.
- When your front wheels draw level with the rear wheels of the car beside which you've stopped, feed your steering wheel *gently* to the left.
- Three *half-turns* of the steering wheel will usually be enough to steer you correctly in towards the kerb.
- You must remember that you don't have right of way and that the front right wing will swing out, so good observation will be crucial.
- Before your left rear wheel touches the kerb, you must change the steering lock to the right so that the front left (near-side) wing moves towards the kerb.
- Then you must straighten up and stop.
- Put on the handbrake and go into neutral and, assuming that your test is over, switch off the engine.
- Don't forget to check in your mirror and look over your right shoulder *before* opening your door.

The reversing manoeuvre is not a speed test, but do learn to move carefully and reasonably smartly. It is adviseable to practise parking behind a single vehicle, at first. As your skill improves, practise parking between two parked vehicles which are a good distance apart. Then try the real thing, where the two vehicles are just a car length apart! Be watchful at every stage and consider getting someone, who knows what they are at, to guide you into the parking spot until you become really proficient.

Turnabout/Turning in Three Points or More

Turnabout is not necessarily a three point turn. You may use five or more moves. However, if you practise and if the space allows, three moves should be enough. The tester is looking for confident and competent handling of the car. So don't panic if you need to use five or more moves.

Get to know the length of your vehicle. Notice the overhang, i.e. the distance between the wheels and the front and rear of the vehicle. You are not allowed to bump the kerb or drive onto the footpath, but you should use the full width of the road. Observe carefully. Show consideration for other road users. Travel at a reasonable speed and be in control at all times. If the camber on the road is steep, rolling towards the kerb is always a possibility. You may use the handbrake after you move forwards or backwards to prevent you bumping the kerb. Roll down your window and give yourself a better view, if you wish.

Let's look at the three points of the turnabout and how you might execute them:

Point One

- Position your vehicle close to the kerb. Don't bump the kerb!
- Apply the handbrake and go into neutral.
- Select first gear and let off the handbrake.
- Check the mirror, signal and check again.
- Look over your right shoulder, as you move off.
- Start turning the steering wheel to the right as you move. By the time you reach the centre of the road, you should have the full right lock on.
- As you approach the opposite kerb, put the left lock on. This will help you when it's time to reverse.
- You may use the handbrake so that you don't roll and bump the kerb.
- Look right, left and right again.
- Start point two, when *it's safe to do so!*

Point Two

- Choose reverse gear and release the handbrake *if* you have applied it.
- Don't roll forward now and bump the kerb!
- Keep a good look out as you reverse towards the kerb you started from.
- Lock the steering wheel to the left.
- Before you stop to apply the handbrake, you may apply the lock to the right. Don't bump the kerb!
- If you want, look out the window to see how close to the kerb you are.
- Apply the handbrake, if necessary. Rewind your window *before* starting to move off.
- Now you are ready for point three.

Point Three

- Select first gear again and indicate.
- Let off the handbrake, *if* you have applied it.
  Be careful now not to roll backwards.
- Move forward, *if it's safe to do so.*
- Put on the right lock as you move towards the opposite kerb.
- Move into the left lane and drive on unless the Tester says otherwise.
- Check your mirror again.

So the procedure for steering lock during turnabout is:
On point ONE – Right lock, left lock.
On point TWO – Left lock, right lock.
On point THREE – Right lock and straighten up.

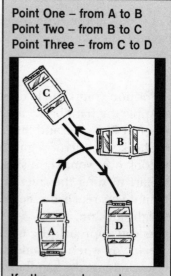

Point One – from A to B
Point Two – from B to C
Point Three – from C to D

If the roadway is very narrow, it may be necessary to repeat Points two and three.

During this manoeuvre, you may have to allow traffic coming from either direction to pass you. Show courtesy and consideration and acknowledge the patience of other motorists, if they choose to wait and let you complete your manoeuvre. If it is appropriate, you may insist that they pass you. Manoeuvre smartly and avoid unnecessary delays. Try out various locations where the roadway is reasonably wide and where it is narrow. Practise the turnabout over and over so you'll gain confidence and competence.

Hill Start

Moving off will mostly be on level roads, but you will also be expected to move away on a hill. This is to show that you can move away correctly from a kerb on an incline, showing co-ordination and clutch control. The tester will ask you to park at the kerb on a hill. Remember the M/S/M/M drill. When you have stopped, apply the handbrake *before* going into neutral. Switch off the engine. You may be asked to demonstrate the hand signals at this point.

Hand Signals

There are three signals for other traffic and three for a person directing the traffic. Test yourself:

For Other Traffic:	For a Garda on Point Duty:
I intend to move off or turn right.	I intend to turn left.
I intend to turn left.	I intend to turn right.
I intend to slow down, or stop.	I intend to go straight on.

 15 & 16

Back to the Hill

Procedure for Hill Start:
- Rewind your window, if you have just demonstrated the hand signals.
- Turn on ignition and select FIRST GEAR.
- Prepare to move away from the kerb. Because you are on a hill, you will need to press the accelerator more than usual.
- *Listen* to the engine as you ease up the clutch pedal.
- The engine sound will change as the revs die down (the biting point).
- MIRROR, SIGNAL, MIRROR, and LOOK OVER RIGHT SHOULDER.
- At this point, release the handbrake, ease the clutch up fully and drive off, *if it is safe to do so.*

Starting off downhill there are some minor changes in procedure.

Procedure for Downhill Start:
- Turn on ignition and select FIRST or SECOND GEAR.
- Prepare to move away from the kerb. Because you are on a downhill slope, you will need to press the footbrake and hold it down.
- *Listen* to the engine as you ease up the clutch pedal.
- The engine sound will change.
- MIRROR, SIGNAL, MIRROR, LOOK OVER RIGHT SHOULDER.
- At this point release the handbrake, but hold down the footbrake until it is safe to drive off.
- Release the footbrake and *then* let the clutch fully up. Little acceleration will be required and you may need to 'cover' the brake on steep hills.
- Take extra care not to cut out on vehicles coming up behind you as it is more difficult to slow down or stop on a hill than on the level.

Parking on a Hill

If you find that you have to park and leave your vehicle on a hill you may take the following safety precautions:

Parking uphill

Leave the vehicle in first gear with the handbrake fully engaged and the front wheels turned right, away from the kerb, if there is one. Sometimes there may no kerb, so leave the wheels turned left, in towards the side of the road.

Parking downhill

Whether or not there's a kerb, leave the vehicle in reverse gear with the handbrake fully engaged, front wheel turned left, in towards the side of the road.

Parking an automatic

If you drive an automatic, point the front wheels towards the kerb with the handbrake fully engaged and the gear-select in the PARK position. This applies for uphill and downhill parking.

The Road Traffic Regulations and You

The Road Traffic (Traffic and Parking) Regulations, 1997 and 1998 set out prohibitions and restrictions on parking. These regulations are enforced by the Gardaí and traffic wardens.

Road authorities are empowered to make bye-laws governing the type of paid parking to be applied in their areas, e.g. disc parking or meter parking. ▽ROTR 45 – 48

Fixed penalty notices ('on the spot fines') were introduced to discourage a wide range of minor traffic violations (illegal parking; speeding; stop sign, yield sign and traffic light infringements; box junction violations; defective tyres; non-wearing of safety belts; breaches of centre roadway and merging/diverging road markings etc.) without necessarily taking up the time of the courts and of the Gardaí in servicing court prosecutions.

Fines range from £15 to £50 depending on the offence and by paying them, motorists avoid court proceedings being instituted against them.

It is also worth noting that a substantial fine and/or a term of imprisonment may be imposed on a person found guilty of undergoing or attempting to undergo the driving test for someone else.

▽ROTR 8, 9, 11 – 14

No Parking

Parking prohibited during times shown

Clearway; stopping or parking prohibited during times shown

Parking prohibited during business hours

No parking at any time

National Car Test

Car testing, which is a requirement under EU law, is being introduced in Ireland on 4th January 2000 and will be carried out by the National Car Testing Service. Its introduction will enhance road safety and environmental protection. Cars will be liable to testing when they are four years old, and every second year thereafter.

The items to be tested include braking systems, steering, windscreens/window glass, lamps and electrical equipment, axles, wheels and suspensions, chassis and attachments, bodywork, safety belts, warning devices, speedometer, noise, and air pollutant emissions. Full details of the test will be documented in a car tester's manual due for publication mid-Summer 1999.

The Motor Tax Office will not tax a car unless it has passed the test.

Part 5: Your Driving Test

Notification

You'll receive notification of the date, time and place of your driving test about six weeks beforehand. Check these very carefully. You will probably feel very nervous, yet if you have prepared well, know the Rules of the Road and how to put them into effect, and have taken at least one pre-test run, then you should have no cause for concern. It makes little sense, though, to approach your local school of motoring for a pre-test run the day before your test, as you may have acquired some bad driving habits. It is unlikely that these will be completely eliminated in a single lesson.

Your Tester

Many people fail their driving test the first time because they expect to fail. Driver testers are officials of the Department of the Environment. They undergo a special training course so that they each know how to classify faults in the same way and to a uniform standard. Their work is supervised and sometimes a supervisory driver tester may sit in on a driving test to monitor the standard of testing. The supervisor's presence will have no bearing on the outcome of your test. Testers are businesslike in their approach, which many candidates find disconcerting. The tester's job is to see that you can carry out the schedule of manoeuvres specified. Do this competently, confidently and safely, with proper regard for other road users, and you will pass.

When you receive notification of your driving test read all the information given carefully. It is quite common for driving test candidates to turn up at the testing centre on the wrong day or at the wrong time. If you intend to take a course of pre-test lessons you should book in with your local instructor right away. It makes little sense to book some lessons the day before your test, as you may not be as ready as you think!

Knowing the Test Area

It is to your own advantage to know the test area and to have driven around it a few times. Many instructors give lessons in and around test areas. On the day of the test, drive around the area again a good hour or so before your test. This will give you a chance to warm up and get your nerves under control. It will also give you a chance to check your car again. But no matter how well you know the test route, it is impossible to predict exactly what traffic conditions will be like during your test, and routes are changed from time to time.

Test Procedure

You should arrive at the driver testing centre shortly before your appointment. Park legally and safely near the centre. Enter the waiting room, if there is one. Show your appointment card and give your name to the official in charge. Presently the tester appointed to carry out your test will call you and invite you to sign a declaration that your vehicle is roadworthy and insured. Your provisional licence will be checked to make sure it is current and valid.

The first part of your test will consist of some oral questions on the Rules of the Road. You will also be asked to identify some road signs. Your answers should be detailed and accurate. If you are nervous you may find that your mind goes blank. To help you overcome this there is a Quiz in the centre of this book.   ▽ROTR 65 – 68

Get someone to ask you these and other questions, and practise saying the answers aloud. The Quiz, though, is no substitute for close study of the Rules of the Road. You should make constant use of the cross-references to the Rules of the Road throughout this text. You will not be asked any 'trick' questions. But if, out of nervousness, you were to answer some of the questions incompletely or incorrectly you can still pass the test. If, by good and careful driving, you show that you can put the Rules of the Road into effect, then you should pass.

You will be asked to lead the way to your vehicle. Be courteous and allow the tester to sit in first. When you sit into your vehicle, carry out the Six Point Check (see page 17). Your tester will tell you that, in your own interest, there will be no unnecessary conversation between you. Don't be concerned about this – it's nothing personal!

You will be told to follow a particular route away from the driver testing centre. You'll drive on the straight for a short while to let you settle down – testers are human too! They know that you are likely to be nervous. You'll be directed through a series of left- and right-hand turns, including negotiating traffic lights and probably a roundabout The test route will be 5miles (8km) approx. You will also have to reverse, make a turnabout and do a hill start. The tester will make notes throughout. Don't allow this to unnerve you. It is normal procedure. (Practice tests with your instructor will prove useful in this regard!)

All instructions should be quite clear, but if you are unsure of what is required you should ask! You may also request that an instruction is repeated. Listen carefully and act according to instruction. If you are told to turn left and you turn right, you will not necessarily fail the test. If you suddenly realise that you have made a mistake try not to become flustered, as you may lose concentration. This could cause you to make errors which would incur test faults.

When your test is complete you will be directed back to the centre, where you first started. You will then be told whether or not you have passed. All in all, the test should take 40 minutes.

During the driving test your driving should be smooth.
Think your actions through and
try not to give your tester any frights.

How You Are Assessed

The driver tester has a special form [Form K] which lists all the points of driving procedure which may be observed during your Test. If faults are observed, they are marked in the following ways:

| X | shows that you have committed a serious fault. A serious fault is anything which shows that you cannot control your vehicle with due regard for your own safety or the safety of other road users.

| ☐ | shows that you have committed more than one serious fault or that the same serious fault has been repeated. A series of serious faults will mean failure.

| O | shows a disqualifying fault. A disqualifying fault is incurred if you do something which is either dangerous or potentially dangerous. Once you incur a fault like this you have failed the test no matter how good your driving is after that.

Reasons for Test Failure

According to the Driver Testing Section of the Department of the Environment there are several common faults which lead to test failure. These include:

- Lack of proper observation.
- Lack of control while steering, changing gears etc.
- Incorrect road position when approaching a turn or a bend.
- Incorrect position on a turn or a bend.
- Incorrect position leaving a turn or a bend.
- Incorrect position on a right-hand turn.
- Failure to use the rear-view mirror.
- Failure to signal or signalling too late.
- Failure to obey road signs and/or road markings.
- Failure to yield right of way or to react correctly to hazards.
- Failure to stop at a STOP sign.

Most test failures seem to result from a series of separate faults or a pattern of similar faults, rather than a single fault like failure to stop at a STOP sign. You cannot fail because of anything you have done before the test. Your test is based on the tester's observation of your driving during it.

When You Pass

When you pass, you will be given your Certificate of Competency. It is valid for 24 months. If it is lost or destroyed you can get a duplicate, but you must satisfy the issuing authority that you have a valid reason for getting a replacement. So, it is adviseable to apply immediately for your Full Driving Licence because if you allow your Certificate of Competency to expire it will not be replaced. You will then have to take another test.

Your Certificate of Competency will note any important extra information, which will be included on your Licence, e.g. 'Must wear corrective lenses', 'Limited to vehicles adapted for disability of Licensee' or 'Limited to vehicles with automatic transmission'. You will naturally be very pleased with yourself, relieved and probably very excited. It is not wise to drive in a state of high excitement. Your driving is likely to be erratic, so remove your L-plates and take a few minutes to compose yourself before making the journey home.

> **Sounding the horn, flashing your headlights, putting on indicators or hazard warning lights do not confer Right of Way.**

If You Fail

If you are told that you have failed, you will probably be upset and disappointed. You will be given a copy of Form K. This is the Report of Driving Test Form which outlines your driving faults as observed by your tester. You will also receive a copy of *The Driving Test*. This is an official guide to the test prepared by, and available from, the Department of the Environment.

The tester is not allowed to discuss the details of your test with you, so when you first examine the Report you may not be able to interpret it. You may not remember where any of the particular faults marked occurred. Careful examination of the form will prove useful to you and your instructor as you prepare to take the test again. Re-apply for the test as soon as possible and be determined to pass the next time, when you will have a different tester. It is unwise to drive when you are upset, so give yourself time to gather your thoughts before setting out.

Lodging an Appeal

If you feel hard done by and that you have a genuine case, you may appeal to the District Court. The personnel in the driver testing centre will be able to give you details about how this is done. The court may refuse your appeal, but if it is satisfied that your test was not carried out properly, you will be given another test. You will not have to pay another fee. On repeating the test you may be observed by a supervisory driving tester.

You can fail the test either for driving over-cautiously or for travelling faster than is safe in the circumstances. You will incur test faults for exceeding the speed limit.

Disabled Drivers

Modern vehicles can be adapted to suit the needs of most physically disabled people. There are two main organisations which deal with needs of disabled drivers. The Disabled Drivers Association of Ireland (DDAI) and The Irish Wheelchair Association (IWA) can assess and advise disabled drivers who are new to driving, or those who are newly disabled and who want to drive.

Disabled Drivers Association of Ireland

Head Office: Ballindine, Co. Mayo. Tel: 094 64054/64266
e-mail: ability@iol.ie
Cork Office: 6 South Terrace, Cork. Tel: 021 313033

The Irish Wheelchair Association

Head Office: Voluntary Social Services Agency,
24 Blackheath Drive, Clontarf, Dublin 3. Tel 01 8335366.
e-mail: info@iwa.ie

Cork Office: Sawmill Street, Cork. Tel: 021 966544

Donegal Office: Manorcunningham Day Centre, Letterkenny, Co. Donegal. Tel: 074 57393

Galway Office: Cul Ard, Wellpark, Galway. Tel: 091 771549

Kilkenny Office: Parnell Street, Kilkenny. Tel: 056 62775

Limerick Office: Unit 5, Mungret Gate, Limerick. Tel: 061 313691

When it comes to the driving test, disabled drivers are generally tested by a supervisory driving tester. The driving test is the same for disabled drivers as it is for everyone else. A Certificate of Competency is only granted to those who deserve it.

Heavy Goods Vehicles

The main emphasis of this text is on the driving test for car drivers, but much of it also applies to drivers of heavy goods vehicles (HGVs) and public service vehicles (PSVs). There are differences between the driving tests for these vehicles and for motor cars, but it is now necessary to have a full B or C1 category licence before you can take the test for category C, D1 or D. There are age restrictions also and more technical information is required of test candidates. This is best acquired on a specialised training scheme run by a reputable driving school or FÁS. ▽ᴿᴼᵀᴿ **5, 6 & 7**

The Motorcycle Test

The Motorcycle Test consists of the same legal preliminaries relating to roadworthiness and insurance as for other vehicles. (A current road tax disc must be displayed on your vehicle.) There is also an oral test on the Rules of the Road and recognition of road signs. ▽ᴿᴼᵀᴿ **51 & 52**

The tester will ask you to lead the way to where the motorcycle is parked. You will then be advised of the test route. If you are unsure of any of the instructions you have been given, you may ask to have them repeated. Memorise them carefully and carry them out to the best of your ability. The tester will observe as you carry out the instructions you have been given.

Correct Procedure

Correct procedure for motorcyclists will involve:

- Looking behind before moving off, changing lanes, overtaking, turning right or left, slowing down or stopping, and correct driving at roundabouts.
- Giving the correct hand signals as well as using the direction indicator. This must be done *clearly and in good time,* while keeping the motorcycle under control. Both hands must be on the handlebars during a turn.

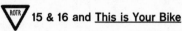 ▽ᴿᴼᵀᴿ **15 & 16 and <u>This is Your Bike</u>**

Compare the hand signals shown by the motorcyclist on page 51 with those shown on pages 15 and 16 of the *Rules of the Road*. It is safer for a motorcyclist to signal while keeping the elbow close to the body.

Several manoeuvres will be required to show that you can negotiate your machine through traffic and handle it capably and safely, while putting the Rules of the Road into effect.

You will be expected to:
• Move off from the kerb.
• Drive at a slow/walking pace for a distance to show balance and control.
• Perform a U-turn properly, observing and signalling correctly.
• Steer a pre-determined course correctly.

When you return to the test centre you'll be told if you've passed or not.

Motorcycle Training

Few motoring schools provide motorcycle tuition and in spite of calls to make motorcycle training compulsory, local authority schemes are not yet widely available. However, in recent years, Dublin County Council has been running a 'Star Rider' course for motorcyclists. It provides training for beginners, intermediate and advanced riders. There are four training centres – Skerries, Baldoyle, Clondalkin and Dundrum, at present.

These courses are really worthwhile, as everyone who has taken one of these courses has passed the Motorcycle Test. The bronze four-hour course is £20, while the silver and gold courses each last twelve hours and cost £60 and £72 respectively. (Costs current at time of printing.) For information contact:

Dublin County Council
Road Safety Section,
Star Rider Courses
Tel: 01 8727777

Safety Precautions

You must always be aware of the need for safety on the roads.

- **Always** maintain your motorcycle properly. Your life and perhaps the lives of others depend on it!
- **Always** wear proper protective clothing and footwear.
- **Always** wear a properly fitting, well-maintained helmet.
- **Always** wear a flourescent Sam Browne or tabard.
- **Always** drive with your headlights on, even during the day.
- **Always** remember that you have a very narrow profile. Other road users may not easily see you.
- **Always** keep within the speed limit.

- **Never** carry a passenger unless you and they are properly insured. Provisional licence holders may only carry a fully qualified pillion passenger. If in doubt – check it out! 51
- **Never** weave in and out of traffic.
- **Never** stay within another driver's blindspot for longer than necessary.
- **Never** overtake a vehicle which has indicated a right turn.
- **Never** come up on the inside when a vehicle has indicated a left turn. This applies especially when coming up behind left turning buses and heavy goods vehicles.

The National Safety Council

The National Safety Council of Ireland has produced a number of very useful leaflets and booklets dealing with road safety. Three in particular are worth mentioning. They are:
1. *A Licence to live?* (Deals with motoring safety)
2. *This is your Bike* (Very useful guide for motorcyclists)
3. *Road Safety for the Farming Community.*

For further information contact:
The National Safety Council of Ireland,
4 Northbrook Road, Ranelagh,
Dublin 6.
Tel: 01 4963422   Fax: 01 4963306
e-mail: info@national-safety-council.ie
www.national-safety-council.ie

Conclusion

Don't presume that you will fail the test on your first attempt. The driving test is quite straightforward. At present the Irish driving test is less demanding than in other EU countries. Test candidates will soon be required to take a written theory examination as well as the oral and practical tests.

As with any examination, knowledge of the curriculum, memorisation of the rules, and familiarisation with the procedures are keys to success. So, on the day of your driving test it will all be up to you! Your knowledge of the Rules of the Road, the instruction you have received, your practice and preparation will pay dividends.

Concentrate on good, safe driving rather than the fact that you are on test and there is no reason why you should not pass – *first time!*

Good Luck!

Answers to Rules of the Road Quiz

1. (a) Unguarded level crossing. 43 & 44
   (b) Steep descent ahead.
   (c) Low bridge ahead. Vehicle height restriction.
   (d) School Ahead – Children crossing.
   (e) Roundabout ahead. 33 & 34

2. Green, Amber, Red, Flashing Amber, Green. ▽ROTR 55 & 56

3. A Garda; A School Warden; persons in charge of animals; pedestrians who have begun to cross or who are on a Zebra or Pelican crossing and flagmen at roadworks or other obstructions.
   ▽ROTR 8, 49, 50 & 54

4. You may not park in a prohibited area or in any place which could cause danger or inconvenience to other road users.
   ▽ROTR 45 – 48

5. A broken yellow line marks the edge of the carriageway and indicates a hard shoulder. ▽ROTR 18

6. (a) A Regulatory sign, i.e. Red circle, white background, black arrow pointing up with a red bar through it.

   (b) A solid white line (nearest you) with a broken white line behind it across the width of the roadway. ▽ROTR 35

7. You must dip your headlights when: meeting or following other traffic; within and outside speed limit areas where the lighting is good; at the start and end of lighting up time; in poor visibility, i.e. fog or falling snow and to avoid inconvenience to others.
   ▽ROTR 40

8. Stop your vehicle! Keep your vehicle at the scene of the accident for a reasonable length of time. ▽ROTR 63 & 64

9. (a) White zig-zag lines at a pedestrian crossing mean no parking or overtaking within the markings. You may stop in the course of traffic or to allow people to cross.

   (b) Yellow zig-zag lines may be found near a school entrance. They mean parking is prohibited. 25, 47 & 54

10. You may only cross if there is a broken white line to the left (your side) of it, in an emergency or to gain access. 18

11. This indicates the area in which parking is prohibited at a bus stop, taxi rank or loading area. 47

12. Overtake on the left if the driver ahead intends going right and you're going straight ahead or left; if you've indicated that you're turning left; if traffic in your lane is moving faster than traffic in the lane to your right. 25

13. You normally overtake on the right and only when it is safe and legal to do so. 25

14. (a) At a junction, where the roads are of equal importance, give way to traffic from the right. Turning left at a T-junction, give way to traffic from the right. If turning right give way to traffic coming both ways.

   (b) When turning right give way to traffic coming straight through. Also give way to oncoming traffic turning left at the junction. 36 & 37

15. A flashing amber light means yield to pedestrians who are crossing. Proceed with caution if the crossing is clear. 37

16. Green means go, but you may only proceed if it is safe to do so! 26

17. Always enter a roundabout by turning left, giving way to any traffic already on the roundabout. ▽ROTR **33 & 34**

18. A clearway sign indicates that stopping or parking is prohibited (except for buses and taxis) at stated times. ▽ROTR **46**

19. (a) Major road ahead. Give way, as necessary, to traffic approaching from either direction.
(b) Clearway – restricted parking. (See 18 above.)
(c) Appointed taxi stand – no parking for other vehicles.
(d) No left turn.
(e) End of speed limit area (Max speed 60mph on ordinary roads or dual carriageways, 70mph on motorways. Reduced speed limit for heavy goods vehicles). ▽ROTR **65 – 68**

Scoring:

When calculating your score, allow yourself 5 marks for each question. For questions 1 and 19 you may have 1 mark for each sign you identify correctly. When you go for your driving test you will not be asked as many questions as this. Nor will you be scoring marks out of 100.

If your score is 85 – 100, this is excellent.
If your score is 55 – 85, this is fairly good.
If your score is less than 55, then you really need
to study the *Rules of the Road* very closely.

Index

Miles – Km conversion chart

Miles	Km
10	16
20	32
30	48
40	64
50	80
60	96
70	112